NATIONAL GEOGRAPHIC

KOALAS

PATHFINDER EDITION

By Sandra Markle

CONTENTS

KOALA
Can They Hang

Millions of koalas once lived in Australia. About 100,000 survive today. What's happening to these popular critters?

By Sandra Markle

LAST On?

Wildfires raged in Australia during January 2002. Firefighters struggled against them, but the blazes destroyed 600,000 acres of forest.

The flames' victims included countless koalas. These tree-climbing mammals live only in eastern Australia. But the fire alarms caught the attention of koala lovers around the world.

The wildfires were just part of a larger problem: Forests are vanishing throughout eastern Australia. Cute and popular as koalas are, they're having trouble hanging on.

Picky Eaters

Koalas' problems stem from being picky eaters. These **marsupials** (animals with pouches for carrying babies) like just one thing.

They're hooked on **eucalyptus** (yew kuh LIP tus), an Australian tree. Koalas use their big noses to sniff out tasty eucalyptus leaves.

"If you offered them something else," says zookeeper Jennifer Moll, "they wouldn't know what to do with it. They'd starve before they'd eat a carrot."

For thousands of years, koalas' devotion to eucalyptus trees was actually a good choice. Eucalyptuses were once the most common trees in Australia. Their leaves contain **toxins**, or poisons. So few other animals eat eucalyptus.

That means more food for koalas. Their stomachs have adapted to remove the toxins. Blood carries the toxins to koalas' livers, which get rid of the poison.

AUSTRALIA

Big Appetites

Koalas weigh only twenty pounds. But they gobble almost three pounds of food a day. That's like a sixty-pound kid eating nine pounds a day!

Eucalyptus leaves, you see, aren't very nutritious. So koalas need supersize servings to get enough energy. Bacteria in the marsupials' intestines turn the tough leaves into useful chemicals.

Because they eat so much food, koalas need lots of room. A single animal's **home range**, or territory, often covers several acres. If eucalyptus trees are rare, though, a koala may need dozens of acres to find its meals.

Eucalyptus branches

Junk Food. *Eucalyptus leaves offer little nutrition. So koalas digest their food for days. All that time lets the animals capture each useful chemical.*

Falling Forests. Australia has lost huge amounts of forest in the past 200 years. That means less habitat for koalas and other animals.

Koala Facts and Figures

Length: 25–30 inches
Weight: about 20 pounds
Habitat: eucalyptus forests of eastern Australia
Life Span: 10–14 years

- Eating eucalyptus leaves makes koalas smell like old-fashioned cough drops.
- Koala fur is thickest on the animal's bottom. That protects the koala while sitting on rough branches.
- Koalas communicate by making noises that sound like snores and burps. When frightened, they scream.

Getting a Grip. *Sharp claws help koalas cling to eucalyptus trees.*

Baby on Board. *An eight–month–old joey, or baby, hitches a ride. In a few more months, the joey will leave its mother.*

5

Pieces of a Puzzle

Even eating as much as they do, koalas don't have much energy. So they rest about 20 hours a day. That doesn't leave them much time to search for mates.

For the population to multiply, koalas must be part of a **colony**, or group. Within a colony, the animals' home ranges fit together like pieces of a puzzle. Koalas generally live alone, but colony members form small groups at mating time.

Five or so weeks after mating, koala mothers give birth. Each mother has a single joey, or baby. Blind and hairless, joeys are no bigger than jelly beans. Like kangaroos, koalas keep their joeys in pouches.

After six months, joeys are strong enough to crawl out of their mothers' pouches. But they don't go off on their own until they're about a year old. Then it's time for the young koala to find its own "puzzle piece" to call home.

But what happens when the puzzle starts to lose pieces?

Lost Puzzle Pieces

Like koalas, humans live in eastern Australia too. Also like koalas, people need room—for houses, farms, malls, parking lots, and so forth. To get space, Australians cut down trees.

Humans have destroyed 80 percent of the forests where koalas once lived. Imagine having only 20 pieces of a 100-piece puzzle. It wouldn't be a pretty picture. Now imagine a male koala trying to find a female whose home range is on the other side of a highway. Or picture a koala losing half its food supply to a parking lot.

Like those stray puzzle pieces, the remaining bits of eucalyptus forest are scattered. That makes it much harder for koalas to gather during mating season. And there's nowhere to go if food runs out—or a fire starts.

As a result, the koala population has plunged. The Australian Koala Foundation (AKF) estimates that there were ten million koalas before 1788. That's when Europeans began moving to Australia.

No one knows exactly how many koalas survive today. The AKF counts about 100,000. Other experts believe only about 40,000 remain.

What Happens Next?

What does the future hold for koalas? Can humans find ways to help them hold on? Australians hope so. "The koala," an Australian once said, "is essential to how we see ourselves."

To protect koalas, Australia has created reserves, or safe places. Wildlife workers have also moved some koalas to less crowded areas. New colonies have formed—an encouraging sign.

Saving koalas is possible. But it will take time, work, hard choices—and plenty of eucalyptus leaves.

Sign of Progress? *Cars kill some 2,500 koalas each year. But signs and speed bumps may help drivers be more koala-friendly.*

Starting Over. *Wildfire damaged this eucalyptus tree, but new growth appeared soon afterwards.*

Forests After Fires

Strange as it sounds, fire can actually *help* eucalyptus forests. Thick bark protects the trees from most flames. And the heat even makes eucalyptuses grow faster!

Blazing Battle. *Fifteen thousand firefighters struggled against Australian wildfires in early 2002. Still, the flames destroyed 600,000 acres of forest.*

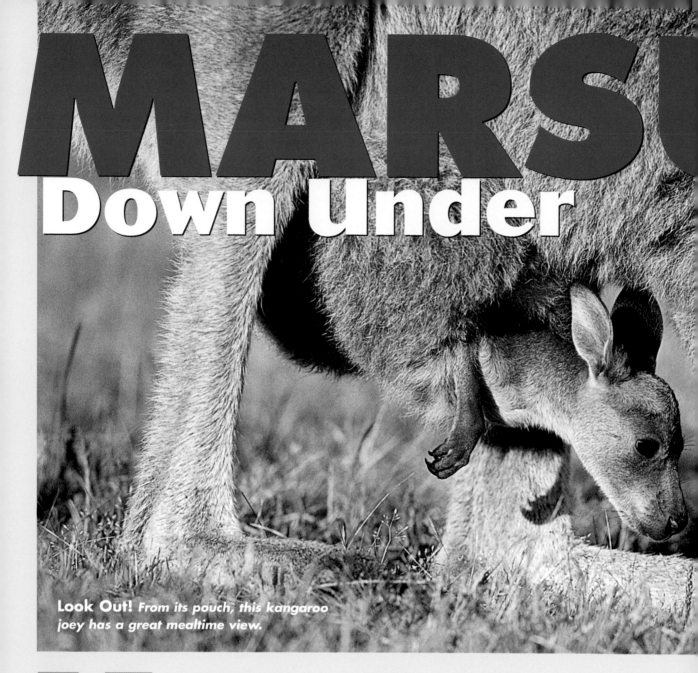

MARSU
Down Under

Look Out! *From its pouch, this kangaroo joey has a great mealtime view.*

Koalas might be Australia's most famous marsupials. Yet many other marsupials also call Australia home. More than 100 different kinds—from kangaroos to quolls—live in this "land down under." Many of them are not found anywhere else.

Marsupials are mammals. Like most other mammals, marsupials have backbones and hair. Marsupial moms give birth to live babies. They feed their babies milk. Yet marsupials do some things differently from other mammals. The biggest difference is how moms care for their young.

Baby on Board

Most mammal babies spend a long time inside their mothers. They are strong the minute they are born. But not marsupials. When they are born, these tots are tiny. It will be months before they can survive on their own.

How do marsupial moms care for their bean-size babies? Most carry them in special pouches. After a baby is born, it crawls into the mother's pouch. The baby lives inside the pouch. There it drinks milk and gets bigger.

For months, the baby travels everywhere with its mom. Then it leaves the pouch and finds its own food. Before long, the young marsupial will make its own way in the world.

JPIALS

Getting a Jump on Life

Kangaroos are marsupials with spring in their step. Their powerful back legs let them leap from place to place. The largest kangaroos can jump 30 feet in one bound. The fastest reach speeds of 34 miles an hour!

There are more than 50 kinds of kangaroos. An adult red kangaroo stands as tall as six feet and weighs almost 200 pounds. Other kinds of kangaroos are as small as rabbits.

Joeys, or baby kangaroos, are only an inch long at birth. But they grow fast. In a few months, a joey can lean out of its pouch. It sniffs at the grass, then takes its first bite. Soon the kangaroo joey hops on its own two legs.

Spotting Danger. *The quoll is one of Australia's many marsupials. Its spots help it hide on the forest floor.*

Pouch–free.
Numbats are one of the few kinds of marsupials without a pouch.

Marsupial Meals

Kangaroos are herbivores. They eat nothing but plants. Other marsupials prefer a diet of bugs or meat. Some eat whatever they can find.

The numbat adores termites. Sluurrrppp! Its long tongue scoops up a trail of tasty treats. With 52 chompers, the numbat has plenty of teeth to help it chew.

One thing numbats don't have is a pouch. Numbat babies hang tightly onto their mom's belly hair instead. As the babies get bigger, their mother digs a burrow. When she goes to hunt, she stows her young safely inside.

Another meat-lover is the Tasmanian devil. This fiendish marsupial is a scavenger. It eats mostly what others have killed. But don't be fooled. The little devil has sharp teeth and claws—and a nasty temper too.

Lucky for you, they don't live just anywhere. Their home is the island of Tasmania off the coast of Australia.

Digging Down Under

Australia is home to most of the world's marsupials. Many thrive in this land down under. But the story isn't that simple.

Take the wombat. This marsupial has small eyes, thick fur, and a stubby little tail. It looks like a miniature bear. Wombats are champion diggers. Some of their tunnels are more than 60 feet long. Wombats sleep and raise their young in these underground burrows.

It's a good system. The burrows protect wombats from heat, cold, rain, and bushfires. Yet wombats still face a serious threat—extinction. Two of the three kinds of wombat are in danger of dying out.

That's true for other marsupials too. Some, like kangaroos, are thriving in the wild. Others, like koalas, are struggling to survive. But there is always reason for hope. After all, even as babies, marsupials are experts at hanging on.

A Devilish Critter.
Unlike most marsupials, the Tasmanian devil eats meat.

Burrow Crazy.
Wombats take digging seriously. Their burrows reach 60 feet or more!

Marsupials

It's time to chew on some questions to see how much you've learned.

1 Why do koalas need to eat so much food each day?

2 Why are eucalyptus trees important to koalas?

3 How is a koala's colony important?

4 What makes marsupials different from other kinds of animals?

5 How are numbats different from other marsupials? How are they the same?